Margaret Thatcher

First Woman Prime Minister of Great Britain

by Leila Merrell Foster

CHILDRENS PRESS®
CHICAGO

To my sister, Mary Virginia Fox

Quotations on pages 10, 13-14, 15, 16, 18, 20, 21, 24, 34, 36, 42, 43, 52, 58-59, and 67 taken from MARGARET THATCHER: FROM CHILDHOOD TO LEADERSHIP by George Gardiner. Published by William Kimber Ltd part of Thorsons Publishing Group, Wellingborough, England.

PICTURE ACKNOWLEDGMENTS

AP/Wide World Photos—pages 2, 8, 22, 56, 69 (bottom right and top), 70 (top), 71 (2 photos), 73 (2 photos), 75 (bottom)

Reuters/Bettmann Newsphotos—pages 75 (top), 86

Solo Syndication—pages 69 (bottom left), 70 bottom left)

UPI/Bettmann Newsphotos—pages 48, 70 (bottom right), 72 (2 photos), 74 (2 photos), 76, 102

Cover illustration by Len W. Meents

LIBRARY OF CONGRESS
Library of Congress Cataloging-in-Publication Data

Foster, Leila Merrell.
    Margaret Thatcher: (first woman prime minister of Great Britain) / by Leila M. Foster.
        p.   cm. — (People of distinction)
    Includes bibliographical references and index.
    Summary: Follows the life and political career of Great Britain's first female prime minister.
    ISBN 0-516-03269-0
    1. Thatcher, Margaret—Juvenile literature. 2. Women prime ministers—Great Britain—Biography—Juvenile literature. [1. Thatcher, Margaret. 2. Prime ministers.] I. Title. II. Series.
DA591.T47F67   1990
941.085'8'092—dc20
[B]
[92]   90–2209
                                                          CIP
                                                          AC

Table of Contents

Chapter 1

WILL SHE WIN?

"Will she win?" That was the question that members of the Conservative party of the House of Commons of Great Britain asked each other. It was before 4:00 P.M. on February 11, 1975. These Tories, as the Conservatives call themselves, had voted between noon and 3:30 P.M. that day. Their votes would decide who would be the leader of their party. Now they were waiting while the ballots were being counted.

That Margaret Thatcher should be in a position to win this election was unexpected. No woman had ever led one of Britain's major political parties in the seven-hundred-year history of parliamentary government. Her party valued traditions. The leader of the Conservative party had a good chance to become prime minister of Great Britain.

In Great Britain the prime minister is the leader of the majority party in the House of Commons, one of the two houses in the legislature, called Parliament. The prime minister also is head of the executive branch of government.

To run for the position of leader involved risks. Margaret Thatcher had to challenge Edward Heath, the current leader of the Conservatives. Heath had been prime minister from 1970 to 1974. Because the Conservatives did not hold a majority of seats in the House of Commons, Heath was no longer prime minister.

Many Tories were unhappy with Heath's leadership. But Edward Heath had given Margaret Thatcher important appointments to posts in the party in the past, including a cabinet post as secretary of education. If he won and Thatcher lost, she probably could forget about future cabinet appointments. If she lost badly, her political career could be over. Her husband, Denis Thatcher, cautioned her: "You should make sure you're able to make a good showing. If you go down badly then you'll be slaughtered afterwards, that's for sure."[1]

Why would she risk it? Mrs. Thatcher was disappointed with the way the Conservative party was being run. They had lost the election in 1974. Their opposition, the Labour party, had won five more seats in Parliament than the Tories had. There was much dissatisfaction within the Conservative ranks. The Tory members of Parliament had won an agreement from their leadership that they should have a vote for a new leader shortly after any general election defeat. The supporters of Edward Heath had agreed to this ballot because they thought he would win easily.

Margaret Thatcher expected others to challenge Heath. However, other possible contenders were blocked for one reason or another. When the friend that she had thought would try for this office decided for family reasons not to do so, Mrs. Thatcher was forced to make a decision whether she would challenge Heath. She lacked the experience of some of the others. The established professionals of the party seemed to favor retaining Heath. Yet the rank and file of the party were clearly unhappy with some of the strategies that he had adopted. Moreover, Margaret Thatcher, when she held the cabinet appointment as minister of education, used to tell women teachers that they should apply for leadership positions: "You cannot go so far up the ladder, and then not go to the limit, just because you are a woman."[2]

Margaret Thatcher was not sure that she could win this election. But she felt that someone's name had to be on the slate with Edward Heath's. It was an opportunity to use the new ballot for a leadership contest. Many Conservatives were willing to admit past mistakes and start with new policies. If Mrs. Thatcher's name were put up as a challenger, she would be someone for whom to vote. Her friends told her that, based on their conversations with other Tory members of Parliament, they thought she would make a good showing. They were not certain she could win.

In November 1974 Mrs. Thatcher decided to place her name in nomination. She immediately went to Heath to tell him of her decision to oppose him in the election.

As soon as Margaret Thatcher announced that she would go for the office, backers of Heath began to look for ammunition to use against her. In the summer she had given an interview to a new magazine that provided advice for persons who were about to retire. She had suggested that it would be wise to buy cans of high protein food like ham, tongue, or sardines over a period of years in order to build up a supply, since the cost of food was rising. Her opponents accused her of advising people to hoard food and of being out of touch with attitudes in the country. They thought they had torpedoed any chances she had of winning the election.

Some of the Tories did not like that kind of war on one of their members. They made sure a copy of the magazine was sent to every member of Parliament. It was clear that Mrs. Thatcher had advised against buying in quantity, but had suggested taking advantage of sales as they were offered in the supermarkets. This tactic of Heath supporters made Margaret Thatcher more determined to run for leader.

Meanwhile Mrs. Thatcher continued in her role as one of the party spokespersons in Parliament. A skilled debater, she made a fine attack on the Labour party's tax legislation. The Tory M.P.'s (members of Parliament) applauded her warmly after her speech.

Airey Neave, who became Mrs. Thatcher's campaign manager in the Conservative leadership election, had been checking on the attitudes of the Tory M.P.'s who were the voters in the leader election. He made an appointment to see Heath to warn him that he was unlikely to win the leadership ballot. If Heath would retire before the election, he could avoid a bitter contest. Heath and his backers, as well as many in the press, thought Heath had the votes to win. If he did not make it on the first ballot, then he certainly would on the second ballot after people saw his strength.

In order to be elected leader of the Tory party, the candidate had to get not just a majority of the votes, but also a lead of 15 percent of those eligible to vote over the next highest person. Thus anyone who refused to vote was effectively voting against the leading candidate. Heath needed a majority of at least 139 votes plus a lead of 42 votes over the next highest candidate. If no one won the required number of votes, there would be a second ballot.

At the end of January 1975, Mrs. Thatcher made a speech to the officers of the Conservative party organization in the district from which she was elected to Parliament:

> It is not a particularly easy time for me. Some people, in the Press and outside it, have not hesitated to impugn my motives, to attribute to me political views which I have never expressed and do not hold, and to suggest that the idea of a woman aspiring to lead a great party is absurd—a strangely old-fashioned view, I should have thought!
>
> You can forget all the nonsense about "defence

of privilege"—I had precious little "privilege"
in my early years—and the suggestion that all
my supporters are reactionary Right-wingers.
It seems to me that those who propagate this
idea do Mr. Heath a poor service by implying
that his support lies only on the "Left-wing" of
our party!

This is not a confrontation between "Left" and
"Right." I am trying to represent the deep feel-
ings of those many thousands of rank-and-file
Tories in the country—and potential Conservative voters, too—who feel let down by our party
and find themselves unrepresented in a political vacuum.[3]

How did Margaret Thatcher propose to fill this vacuum?
What was the new platform she wanted the Tories to adopt?
She urged them to turn to traditional ideals such as concern
for individual freedom, opposition to improper use of
government power, support for the right of working people
to pass their earnings on to their children, protection of private property against government takeovers, and the right
of people to work without oppression by employers or union
bosses.

January was also the month in which Mrs. Thatcher made

a speech at a private luncheon club. That speech made the press take her candidacy more seriously. Before then, the reporters had seen her as someone who would keep the voting open until the second ballot, when another candidate would come forward. Now they began to see her as a possible winner.

Then another M.P. entered the race. Hugh Fraser was a person of some standing. For Tories who opposed Heath, but did not want to vote for a woman, Fraser was a candidate to support.

Politicking went on in earnest. Even before the date of the election was announced, Mrs. Thatcher's backers told her that in their poll of the M.P.'s, she was very close to denying Heath a first ballot win. She was surprised that the figures were so favorable and responded: "In that case, let's really go."[4] Every Sunday evening of the campaign, Mrs. Thatcher's team met at her home to plan strategy for the coming week.

The style of campaigning of the two camps was quite different. As leader, Heath had the organization and staff of his office. When he met with the new M.P.'s at dinner parties that were arranged, he focused on the past and made statements justifying his actions from 1970 to 1974 when he was prime minister. He seemed ill at ease.

The Thatcher camp had small offices and few campaign support services. When Mrs. Thatcher met with the new

M.P.'s, she was more relaxed and answered questions rather than made speeches. She described her style of leadership in a letter released on the first of February as one of listening and including others in the dialogue within the party.

> Listen to the younger generation. They don't want equality and regimentation, but opportunity to shape their world, while showing compassion to those in real need.
>
> Listen to working families the length and breadth of Britain. They don't want growing State direction of their lives. They want more say over how the wealth they earn is used, more say over the quality of their children's schooling. More choice, not less.
>
> Listen to men and women at work. They don't want to be propped up by subsidies, but to see their industries profitable, and Britain again the workshop of the world.
>
> To listen and to lead—that is our role. True leadership offers inspiration and hope, but also explains honestly the severe economic constraints under which we work.[5]

Both the Heath and the Thatcher campaign teams took informal polls. Both thought they had a victory. The claim of the Heath campaign team that he would win outright on the first ballot may have forced a few of the M.P.'s who were adopting a "wait and see" attitude to vote for Mrs. Thatcher in order to preserve a chance for a second ballot.

Tuesday, February 4, was the date of the first ballot. Mrs. Thatcher woke up early and cooked breakfast for her husband before he drove off to his office. At 8:00 A.M. her campaign manager telephoned to tell her that according to his figures no one would win, but it was going to be close. With luck she might even come in a little ahead of Heath. At 9:00 A.M., Thatcher drove to Parliament to work on some legislation. She voted before 1:00 P.M. and then left for a luncheon meeting about a finance bill. In the afternoon she returned to her office to await the news. The balloting closed at 3:30 P.M.

Before the vote was counted, Heath's representative bet that his candidate would get more than 130 votes, while Thatcher's representatives bet Mrs. Thatcher would get more than 100. Some 80 Tory M.P.'s waited in the corridor outside the vote-counting room to see what the news might be. When Heath's representative walked out to carry the news to his candidate, he looked shaken. Mrs. Thatcher's representative looked expressionless. Then when the M.P.'s filed into the committee room, the results were announced:

Margaret Thatcher   130
Edward Heath   119
Hugh Fraser   16

First, there was a gasp of surprise, and then a cheer from Mrs. Thatcher's supporters. The reporters waiting outside were shocked by the news.

Airey Neave brought Mrs. Thatcher the news of her vote count. Shortly after that, she met the press and released the statement: "We believe that our vote will remain firm in the second ballot, and we hope to attract a few more."[6]

She still needed to win a clear majority of 139 votes plus 42 votes over her nearest opponent.

When Heath was given the news of the ballot, which was so contrary to what his campaign managers had thought it would be, he responded, "So we got it all wrong."[7] After talking the situation over with his adviser for twenty minutes, Heath resigned—bringing to an end his ten years of party leadership.

With the resignation of Heath, more people rushed to become candidates, because now the risk of offending the current leader was removed. William Whitelaw, who had backed Heath, became a candidate. However, other former Heath supporters were welcomed into the ranks of the Thatcher backers. Jim Prior, Sir Geoffrey Howe, and John Peyton also declared their candidacy. There were rumors that others might join as well. The larger the number of persons on the ballot, the more difficult it would be for one person to get the majority of the votes that were needed. The London bookies favored Whitelaw over Mrs. Thatcher at 4 to 6 odds.

Both Whitelaw and Mrs. Thatcher had been invited to speak at the national conference of the Young Conservatives that weekend. Whitelaw was to talk on party organization, which did not provide the same opportunity for the kind of rousing address that Mrs. Thatcher had in her assignment to deal with economic issues and the need for private enterprise. The thirteen hundred delegates in the youth wing of the Tory party gave her a standing ovation. The television cameras carried this success to an even larger audience who were learning what this now-serious contender for the leadership of the Conservatives might be like.

Whitelaw and Mrs. Thatcher walked together outside the conference hall to get some lunch. The press crowded around them. With cameras snapping, one reporter urged Whitelaw: "Give her a kiss." He did, and that picture was in almost every Sunday paper. In a way the kiss was a symbol for the friendlier contest before the second ballot. The personal attacks of the first ballot were over, and the new contest was one between colleagues who were prepared to work together when the election was over.

The night before the second ballot the campaign leaders gathered to assess their chances. Airey Neave reported that a win was still not certain. The tally he had was 137 for Thatcher, 78 for Whitelaw, 19 for Howe, 11 for Prior, and 9 for Peyton, with 9 doubtful but leaning toward Thatcher and 13 either doubtful or not checked. If some of the doubtfuls voted for her, Margaret Thatcher would have a narrow victory.

When the Tory M.P.'s crowded into the committee room to learn the results of their balloting on February 11, they all wondered if she could win on this ballot. The results were announced:

Margaret Thatcher	146
William Whitelaw	79
Geoffrey Howe	19
James Prior	19
John Peyton	11

She had won her majority with seven votes to spare and was 67 votes in front of Whitelaw. The news spread: "Maggie's done it."

Her campaign manager brought the news to Mrs. Thatcher: "It's all right—you're Leader of the Opposition!"[8] She telephoned her husband, but he had already read the news. She prepared a short message for the press conference that had been arranged in the committee room. When asked to try the microphones in the room, she did not say: "Testing, 1, 2, 3." Instead, she used her victory vote figure: "1, 4, 6."

In her statement, she recalled other leaders of the Conservative party: "To me it is like a dream that the next name in the list after Harold Macmillan, Sir Alec Douglas-Home and Edward Heath is Margaret Thatcher. Each has brought his own style of leadership and stamp of greatness to his task, and I shall take on the work with humility and dedication."[9]

Nine days after her election as leader of the opposition, she was formally elected leader of the Conservative party to the applause of over six hundred persons—M.P.'s, peers, and party representatives.

Margaret Thatcher began her work of unifying the party after her unprecedented win as a woman and as one outside the established power base. She offered Heath an important position on her team, which he declined, arousing speculation that he wanted to be available to be recalled as leader if she stumbled. One of the former Conservative cabinet ministers commented: "The choice of Margaret Thatcher is the greatest gamble in the history of the Tory Party. We will either win magnificently or lose disastrously. I see nothing in between."[10]

Not only did Margaret oust the Labour party from power in the next election, thereby becoming the first woman prime minister, but she has won further elections. She has had the longest consecutive term as prime minister in the modern history of Great Britain—longer than Churchill, Disraeli, and Gladstone, some of the other famous prime ministers.

21

The Roberts family in 1945 included Muriel, Mr. Alfred Roberts, Mrs. Beatrice Roberts, and Margaret.

Chapter 2

HER FATHER'S DAUGHTER

As prime minister of Great Britain, Mrs. Thatcher lives at Number 10 Downing Street, the official residence. It is both an office building and a home. At Number 10 Downing Street, the apartment of the prime minister is on the upper floors. Mrs. Thatcher grew up in a home above her family's grocery store. She has often joked that she is still living above the store.

The home in which Margaret Thatcher was raised is located in Grantham, in Lincolnshire, England. Grantham is a market town, the center for the surrounding farm district. In Mrs. Thatcher's time there, the population was about thirty thousand. Her house was on one of the busy highways and only a little farther away were the railroad yards. She was well acquainted with traffic noises.

The grocery shop was on the ground floor of a brick building that was three stories high. The family lived above. On the third floor Margaret and her older sister, Muriel, each had a small bedroom. There was a small kitchen on the ground floor. The lavatory was outdoors in the yard. The house was furnished with solid furniture, mostly Victorian mahogany. Her father had obtained some of it at auction sales. Here Margaret lived for her first eighteen years.

Mrs. Thatcher, who uses her married name, was born in this home on October 13, 1925, as Margaret Roberts. In Great Britain, where consciousness of social class is strong, it is surprising that the first woman prime minister came from a family of modest circumstances. Margaret's paternal grandfather had been a shoemaker and lived with his wife in a little cottage. Her father, perhaps because of his poor eyesight, did not follow in his father's trade, but left school at age thirteen to go into the grocery business. After a while, he became the manager of a store. During World War I, he and his wife managed to save enough to buy the grocery shop in which everyone in the family worked. Margaret's mother, Beatrice Ethel Stephenson, had trained as a dressmaker. Beatrice's father had worked for the railway. Her mother was a farmer's daughter. Margaret Thatcher is proud of her family:

> I owe everything in my life to two things: a good home, and a good education. My home was ordinary, but good in the sense that my parents were passionately interested in the future of my sister and myself. At the same time they gave us a good education—not only in school, but at home as well.[1]

The family business was more like a country store than the supermarkets of today. Customers, including some of the leading citizens of town, would stop in and talk about the concerns of the town or the nation. Alfred Roberts, Margaret's father, was active in the local Methodist church and was a lay preacher who frequently made visits to other congregations. He was elected to the town council, and in 1945 he became mayor of the town. He was one of the leaders in the local Rotary Club. He regretted that he had not had an opportunity of formal higher education and he engaged in a program of self-education by reading library books.

For the first ten years of Margaret's life, her maternal grandmother lived with the family. Phoebe Stephenson was fond of telling her granddaughters: "If a thing's worth doing, it's worth doing well." And, "Cleanliness is next to godliness."

Both sides of the family were strong Methodists. The girls went to Sunday school twice each Sunday—in the morning and afternoon. They also went with their parents to the morning and evening services. On Tuesday evenings, the girls went to the youth group. Of course, the family participated in church events such as Christmas plays. Margaret once played the role of an angel. When Mrs. Roberts baked, she often made enough to distribute to those in need.

Since games were strictly off-limits on Sundays, Margaret once asked her father why she could not play games the way her friends did. Her father replied that she should not do things just because other people were doing them. She should make up her mind what she was going to do and then persuade people to follow her.

The church also provided a good training in music. Margaret was in the church choir for a while and had a good singing voice. She took piano lessons from age five until fifteen, when the pressure of her schoolwork forced her to stop. She was appreciative of the oratorios and special musical talent that the church brought in once or twice a year.

While the grocery store meant that the children were around their parents more than was the usual case, it also meant separations. One of the parents had to mind the store, so it was rare for the whole family to sit down to a meal together during the week. Also, vacations had to be taken separately. Mrs. Roberts and the girls would go for a week to the nearest holiday resort, Skegness. They went to the same boardinghouse for years. They rented rooms but brought their own food to prepare themselves. At Skegness, there was the fun fair, boating on the lake, and the greatest treat, the music hall show. Margaret's father took his holiday at another time, when the family was home to watch the store. Alfred Roberts did not buy their car, a secondhand Ford, until World War II, so there were very few excursions away from Grantham.

Margaret began her schooling at age five at the Huntingtower Road Elementary School. It was not the closest school to her home, but the one her father considered best. It was about a mile away, and Margaret had to walk it four times a day, since lunches were not served at the school. She did not have a bicycle until she was an adult and earning her own money. While rich people would not have sent their children to a school run by the town council, Margaret's school drew students from a broad social background including children from an orphanage, those whose families were quite poor, and those from merchant families.

Margaret was always near the top of her class and skipped a grade soon after enrolling. When she was ten, Margaret took an examination and received a scholarship to a girls' school. Again she was very good in her studies, except for art. She liked the sports of field hockey and swimming. She was active in the debating and dramatic societies. When the headmistress of her school asked her what career she wanted to follow, Margaret replied that she had been thinking of the Indian Civil Service. Margaret liked the author Rudyard Kipling, who wrote many stories about India. It must have seemed like a glamorous life. The headmistress objected that it was difficult for women to get into that career. Margaret responded that to her it sounded like a good reason for trying to get into it.

Margaret's sister, Muriel, had a pen pal in Vienna named Edith, and Margaret wrote to a girl in France. The parents of Muriel's friend wrote to the Roberts in 1939 asking if the family could help to make a temporary home for their daughter in England. Edith was Jewish and the Nazis controlled Austria and were persecuting Austrian Jews. Edith came to live with the Roberts family, and thirteen-year-old Margaret learned about life under the Nazi occupation from the stories that Edith told.

Winston Churchill became Margaret's hero not only because of his leadership during World War II, but also because of his principles and his earlier stand against appeasement. When there were air raids, the family would sit underneath the dining room table on the first floor since they had no cellar. Margaret used to do her homework there. Perhaps she developed her superb powers of concentration then.

Alfred Roberts involved his daughter in discussions about national and international events. Margaret also helped in some of his political campaigns. She says that she did not think of politics as a realistic career choice for herself then because she had to be able to earn her own way. For politics, you needed an independent source of wealth.

Her sister, Muriel, left home when Margaret was thirteen in order to take a five-year course in physiotherapy. When Muriel returned to work in Grantham, she introduced Margaret to makeup and lipstick.

Margaret began to think about universities to which she

could apply to continue her education. She picked out three or four that were likely choices and filled out her applications. However, her best friend, Margaret Goodrich, was planning to go to Somerville College at Oxford University. Margaret asked herself why she should not try for this university that had more prestige and more to offer her. When she approached the headmistress of her school about the matter, the woman tried to dissuade her from trying for the scholarship examination. There were a number of problems in Margaret's situation—not the least of which was her lack of any knowledge of Latin, a prerequisite for Oxford. Moreover, the headmistress gave the impression that perhaps Margaret was overreaching her station in life.

Margaret went to her father to discuss the problems. Since her school did not teach Latin, her father arranged for her to take a crash course with a tutor to prepare her for the examination. Back Margaret went to report her plan, but the headmistress said that she would not waste the school's money to pay the entrance fee for an exam Margaret was so likely to fail. Margaret returned the next day with a check from Alfred Roberts to pay the entrance fee. She qualified in Latin and went to Oxford to take the examination that involved written papers and an interview. She did very well, but just missed the scholarship. It was awarded to a girl who had tried for it the year before and would not be eligible after that year. Margaret was put on the waiting list for a place at Oxford and was notified at the beginning of the fall term that she would be admitted to study.

She did have some second thoughts about the choice of a major in chemistry. Margaret wondered if she wouldn't have done better to choose law. Her father had encouraged her to watch the court proceedings when she turned sixteen, the age at which she could be admitted to the public galleries. She talked with a lawyer who was one of her father's friends about her question. He told her that he, himself, had a degree in physics. She could take a degree in law after the one in chemistry and be especially qualified in the area of patents.

Chapter 3

CHOOSING A CAREER

Margaret arrived at Oxford just a few days before her eighteenth birthday in 1943. It was a big change from her hometown of Grantham. Oxford was cosmopolitan and sophisticated. The women's colleges, fewer in number than the men's colleges at Oxford, were tough academically. Competition for admission was keener. Socially, there were more rich people than had lived in Grantham. New cultural opportunities were available to Margaret.

She must have experienced something of a shock because of the differences. Margaret was on her own, away from the shelter of her family. She was homesick.

> When you've been at home, you have never known what it's like to be lonely. It's quite an experience the first time you come across it and it takes a while to make new friends.[1]

As a woman and a science student who had lab hours, it was even harder to fit into the patterns of undergraduate life.

Margaret received some scholarship help from a number

of sources. Also, she had the savings that her parents had taught her to accumulate.

When she first arrived at Oxford, it was wartime. Black-outs as protection against air raids and shortages of food put a crimp in the students' social life. Margaret volunteered as a fire watcher and helped out at the armed forces' canteen where she made sandwiches, did the dishes, or served at the counter.

Margaret took advantage of the opportunities Oxford provided. She did not go out for sports because she was not very athletic. However, she joined the Bach Choir, the Scientific Society, and the student Methodist group. Perhaps the most important organization Margaret joined was the Oxford University Conservative Association. She went to its weekly meetings to listen to outstanding invited speakers. She was elected to the Association's committee and later served as its general agent, treasurer, and eventually its president. She was at the top of the Tory organization at the university. Male undergraduates might also belong to the Oxford Union where debates were held every Thursday evening. In Margaret's day, women were not admitted as members but could listen as guests in the gallery. Although it was the only discrimination of which she was aware at Oxford, she was not too upset by it since she found many of the debates good entertainment but lacking in serious quality.

Margaret was a serious person, but she also enjoyed the social life at Oxford. When the war ended, many older students returned to the university. There were more parties. While she and her sister had not gone to dances in Grantham, she came to love ballroom dancing. Later when she took rooms with two other girls, she gave parties that were known for providing good food, drink, and a nice mix of friends.

During her first summer's vacation, Margaret went back to Grantham. There she taught chemistry, mathematics, and general science for six weeks. Because of the war, an August school term was arranged so that the students would be free later in the year to help harvest crops. It was this teaching job that was to pay for her first bicycle—almost a necessity for an undergraduate to get around town. It was perhaps typical of Margaret's honesty that she never held herself up as a teacher based on this six-week stint even when it might have served her purpose when she became minister of education.

Although she was a hardworking and consistent student, Margaret was not tops in her field. She got a good second. (Oxford degrees are classified first, second, and third class.) She did a fourth year of research in the field of X-ray crystallography in order to get an honors degree in science. She would need her job in science in order to allow her to study law, but science was not her first love:

I felt very much how *impersonal* work in the laboratory was. One reason why I was so active in politics was that all the time it's concerned with people. I think a lot of scientists of my generation were looking for ways in which they could apply their knowledge, not in a laboratory, but out in the field.[2]

Politics was Margaret's first love. She enjoyed talking politics with her friends. One of them challenged her: "You'd really like to become an M.P.?" That question made her realize that, yes, she did want to be a member of Parliament. Her Tory ideas when she was at Oxford were pretty close to the center of her party, with no identification with the right-wing group. She collaborated on a paper suggesting that the decolonization of Africa should leave national boundaries as far as possible along the lines of the tribal territories. As far as Conservative policy, Margaret wrote against an over-reliance on reason and logic in setting party platforms.

When Margaret left Oxford, she was recruited by a firm making plastics. About eight or ten university graduates were hired for the research and development department. She started work at a salary of 350 pounds a year—50 pounds less than the male graduates. She lived in a room nearby in Colchester. Of course, she immediately joined the local Conservative association. She enjoyed being part of a group of returning ex-servicemen who met in a pub for political discussions.

In 1948 she attended the Conservative party conference at Llandudno as a representative of the Oxford graduates. Margaret was sitting next to John Grant, a friend from her undergraduate years, and next to him was John Miller, the chairman of the Conservative association from Dartford. Dartford was looking for a candidate to run for Parliament against a popular Labour candidate. Four local men had been asked to take the candidacy but had turned it down. Under the British parliamentary system, the candidate does not have to live in the district. Margaret's friend asked if they would consider a woman. Miller replied that it was a tough industrial area, perhaps not suited for a woman. Grant pressed his question. Miller responded that a woman could apply. Grant suggested that Margaret consider the position. This idea took her by surprise. She had not thought of it before.

While the seat from Dartford was not considered attainable by a Conservative like Margaret, it was a good training ground for a young politician. Furthermore, it was close to London. Some twenty-four persons applied. That number was cut down to three, and from that slate Margaret was chosen. The selection committee was impressed by her ability to take a complicated matter and describe it in simple terms without talking down to her audience.

The choice of the committee was very unusual. Margaret was a woman selected for an industrial area. She was a twenty-three year old going against a veteran politician. She would be expected to deal with issues ranging from questions of raw material purchased by the government to rail transportation to get her constituents to work in London.

The next step after being selected by the committee was for Margaret's name to be presented for adoption to all the members of the Conservative association of that district. Here was the first big political meeting with her constituents, and the impression she would make on people was important. Her father came to speak on her behalf. The meeting was packed with people. She reported: "All sorts of people turned out to see this unusual creature."[3] Even though Margaret was an unusual candidate for that district, she was adopted with enthusiasm with only one vote against her.

That evening she was invited for dinner by some of the leading members of the party. A few days before the dinner, the hostess realized that she would be one man short. The hostess invited Denis Thatcher, a business associate of her husband's. When the question of how Margaret was going to get home was raised, Margaret replied that she was going by train. However, Denis Thatcher invited Margaret to go with him in his car. So it was that she met her future husband.

Even though it was unlikely that she would win her campaign in view of the strength of the incumbent candidate from the Labour party, Margaret set about her campaign with determination. "If a job's worth doing, it's worth doing well." She gave up her work because it was difficult to get to her district. She took a job with a company in London. First, Margaret concentrated on getting to know the leaders in every ward of her district and then directed her efforts to outside organizations. She became involved with local politics and local issues.

The Labour member of Parliament who had the seat that Margaret was after was Norman Dodds. He took an interest in this young and unusual challenger from the Tories. He and Margaret treated each other with respect. In a rather unusual move for a sitting M.P., he even challenged her to a debate. Of course she accepted. Even though he was a very good debater, Margaret held her own. He never challenged her again. Because she was an unusual candidate, she received good press coverage.

An election for Parliament in Britain is held in any of three instances: when the party in power loses a vote of confidence in Parliament, when the party in power calls for an election because it thinks it is the best time to win the most seats in Parliament, or when five years have passed since the last election.

Margaret's first election campaign came in a wet and

snowy winter in 1950. She began her day with a morning conference. Then she went to an open-air meeting at lunchtime. Also, she visited the cafeterias of the local factories. In the afternoon, Margaret went door to door introducing herself. Then she rested up before the one or two evening meetings. Often there would be heckling at such meetings, but she knew that the heckling she received in Dartford was fair game—not the kind that was intended to drown out what she was saying.

Although she lost the election as was expected, Margaret cut the lead of the Labour candidate by twenty thousand votes from the last election. The Conservatives just missed taking over the majority of seats of Parliament. The next election was not to come until October 1951.

Margaret felt tired after the pace of her first campaign. She later reported that perhaps with more experience in campaigning, one developed more stamina and perhaps better planning so that the effort was not quite so exhausting. Nevertheless, she liked politics and made valuable friends both in and out of her district.

After the election, Margaret moved back to London and began studying law. Denis Thatcher also lived in London, and the two continued dating. He was thirty-six years old when he met Margaret, ten-and-a-half years older than she. He was tall and athletic. Denis Thatcher liked music, as Margaret did. He also liked fast cars, which she did not. He was the general manager of a company with an international market that produced paint, marine and agricultural chemicals, and other products. It was a firm partly owned by Denis's family and in which he had worked since 1936.

Denis Thatcher had been married once before. It was a wartime marriage. He had served in the royal artillery in Italy and France. When he was in the army, they had not been able to live together. On his return, they were strangers to each other. The marriage did not survive, and they were divorced in 1946. Denis's first marriage was not general knowledge until Margaret's victory over Heath in 1975. Their twin children were not even aware of the first marriage. Margaret said that there was no effort to keep it a secret: "One didn't keep it a secret he'd been married before. One wasn't asked. One just didn't talk about a thing like that."[4]

Denis Thatcher asked Margaret to his annual trade association dance. His company chairman, observing Margaret, told Denis he should marry her. Denis thought over the advice and on his return from a holiday in France and Spain, he proposed. Margaret accepted. Should they announce their engagement with an election campaign just breaking? They sought the advice of a friend who cautioned against it. Margaret agreed since it might send a signal to her party workers that she had her mind on other things. Since their dating had been in London, the people in Dartford were not aware of their interest in each other. However, the news came out just before the election. As the youngest woman candidate, Margaret received a great deal of publicity about the engagement, but not in time to affect the election results.

Margaret did not win, but she cut the Labour majority by a further thirteen hundred votes. She was gaining on Norman Dodds. With the Conservatives winning a majority of seventeen parliamentary seats and likely not to hold another election for five years, it was time for Margaret to leave Dartford. If she continued in politics, she would look for another district where it was more likely that she could win.

Chapter 4

STARTING A FAMILY

The wedding took place in December of 1951 in the Methodist church, Wesley Chapel, in City Road, London. About fifty guests attended the reception that was held in the home of Mr. Alfred Bossom, the chairman of the Conservatives from Kent. The honeymoon was Margaret's first trip abroad. The couple went to Portugal and Paris, where Denis had some business, and then on to Madeira, before returning to London and the apartment in which Denis had lived.

Two months after her marriage, Mrs. Thatcher was asked to write an article for a Sunday paper. It was to be about the role of women in the new Elizabethan Age that was being discussed because of the coronation of Queen Elizabeth II. Mrs. Thatcher was a promising young politician who was just a few months older than the queen. The ideas that she expressed in 1952 would not seem very radical today, but they probably shook up a few members of the Conservative party. Mrs. Thatcher expressed the hope that with a queen on the throne, prejudice against women would be removed and women would have new opportunities for leadership. She looked forward to seeing more women combine marriage and a career. She asked:

Why have so few women in recent years risen to the top of their professions? One reason may be that so many have cut short their careers when they marry. *In my view this is a great pity.* For it *is* possible to carry on working, taking a short leave of absence when families arrive, and returning later. In this way gifts and talents that would otherwise be wasted are developed to the benefit of the community. *The idea that the family suffers is, I believe, quite mistaken.* To carry on with a career stimulates the mind, provides a refreshing contact with the world outside—and so means that a wife can be a much better companion at home. Moreover, when her children themselves marry she is not left with a gap in her life which so often seems impossible to fill.[1]

She hoped that more women would be active in politics. At that time there were only 17 women out of 624 members of Parliament in the House of Commons. For more women to be in Parliament "and in the highest places, too" would be a good thing for the women of Britain and for the men, too.

Mrs. Thatcher and her husband had a private understanding that made for harmony in their marriage. Their work came first. Mr. Thatcher's job often took him on trips abroad and was important for the support of the family. Mrs. Thatcher turned to her law studies for admission to the bar and to setting up homemaking. She put politics on hold for a while because she felt that if she were properly organized, she could do two things well, but not three.

Just a little more than a year after her marriage, Mrs. Thatcher learned that she was pregnant. Both parents-to-be greeted this news with happiness. Mrs. Thatcher stepped up her legal studies so that she could take her bar intermediate examination before the child was due. She passed that exam in May, but then in August she had a surprise. The baby was supposed to arrive in October, but seven weeks early, twins were born by Caesarian section. The Thatchers had no idea that twins were on the way. Weighing only four pounds each, Mark and Carol joined the Thatcher family.

Mrs. Thatcher decided to proceed with her bar finals in December, and she passed. Her husband boasted: "Bar Intermediate in May, produced twins in August, and Bar Finals in December. I'd like to meet another woman who can equal that record!"[2]

With premature twins to look after, Margaret Thatcher reported that the children were the center of her life. She had help from a children's nurse, because twins wake up at different hours for feeding and require more attention. As the children grew, she followed some of her parents' values and rejected others. She did not bring the children up in the strict religious training she had received, with churchgoing many times a week. She did try to interest them in things around them as her father had interested her. Her sister remembers that Margaret never screamed at the twins, but always tried to reason with them. If the family visited a farm at harvesttime, she wanted the children to learn how the machinery worked. If they went for a boat trip, the children could learn how to crew. She arranged her time so that she could be with the children for play part of each day, and she always read to them before they went to sleep.

Denis praised his wife's domestic talents. As a child, she had learned to sew well. Now she made some of the clothing for the twins—especially dresses for Carol. Her cooking was superb. She liked cooking and giving small dinner parties, and she always strove for perfection in her efforts.

Mrs. Thatcher followed her own advice and did not stop her career just because she had married and had a family. Now that she had passed her exams, she began her work in the British legal system. Lawyers in England are divided into two groups: solicitors and barristers. Solicitors meet with clients and help with legal problems, but may not plead cases in the superior courts. They are not members of the bar. They help to prepare cases for the barristers. Barristers try cases in the courts and are members of the bar. Mrs. Thatcher began her training in various aspects of the law by becoming associated with a firm of barristers. It was at this time that she became acquainted and worked with Airey Neave, who later became her campaign manager. Also, she reached the decision that she did not want to specialize in patent law, but in tax law.

Politics was put to one side while Mrs. Thatcher practiced law and supervised the twins. She did put her name in for a parliamentary seat that had become vacant in 1954 in a district where a Tory was likely to win. A local man was chosen instead. She did not enter any of the races for seats in the 1955 general election. The twins were still quite young. However, she did campaign for other Tory candidates, and the Conservatives increased their majority to sixty seats.

One of the actions of the Tory party was to ease up on rent restrictions. This act affected the Thatcher family a great deal. The rent was so increased on their apartment that they decided that it was time to buy a house. The prices of houses in their section of London were too high, so they opted for a place in Kent. It was near Mr. Thatcher's work, but Mrs. Thatcher had to take the train to London and her office. She drove the twins and some of their neighbors' children to school before going to the train. Other parents picked them up in the afternoon. The Thatchers still employed a nanny for the children.

Mrs. Thatcher enjoyed organizing various outings with the twins in their new home in Kent. Annual family holidays were planned. After trying a number of places, they settled on Seaview on the Isle of Wight. Mrs. Thatcher stayed with the children while her husband joined them for a couple of weeks and on weekends away from his work.

Although she was making a name for herself in tax work and was active in the Inns of Court Conservative Association, Mrs. Thatcher knew that if she wanted to be elected to Parliament she could not sit out many more general elections. Her children would be in school by the time the next election would be likely. Mark was to go to a boarding school when he was nine years old. Margaret Thatcher began to submit her name as a candidate to various selection committees in the area around Kent and London so that she could still be close to her home base. She wanted a district where she would have some chance of winning, as opposed to a district like Dartford that was safe for the Labour party. She was turned down by several committees.

Margaret Thatcher applied for the seat at Finchley with two hundred other hopeful candidates. Finchley was vacant because the incumbent was retiring at the next general election. It was considered a safe Tory seat with a twelve-hundred majority in the last election. It was an outer suburban district made up of many London commuters. For the most part, the people were upwardly mobile with many self-employed and self-made businesspeople. Because there were a large number of Jews in the district, Middle East issues were considered important.

The selection committee narrowed the field from two hundred to twenty-two persons. Then they asked all candidates the same questions and eliminated all but four. One withdrew. The thirty-three-year-old Mrs. Thatcher made the others look too established and too traditional for some of the younger Conservatives in the district. She was selected as their candidate to fight for the seat in Parliament. Although she had written her husband, who was away on a business trip, the letter was not received before he left to come home. Denis first learned about her selection when he was reading a newspaper on the airplane.

Mrs. Thatcher's adoption meeting by the district party went very well. The press was impressed by her grasp of issues and her ability to speak clearly without notes. She had a year or so to campaign before the general election. Again, she approached the task in her thorough manner. Her seat was pretty safe, and the Labour party made some mistakes in the campaign. There was a Tory landslide, with the Conservatives being returned to power with a majority. The results for Finchley were:

Margaret Thatcher (Conservative)	29,697
Eric Deakins (Labour)	13,437
Henry Spence (Liberal)	12,701

Her majority of 16,260 was 3,435 votes higher than that of her predecessor. Margaret Thatcher was now an M.P., a member of Parliament.

Margaret Thatcher, Conservative Member of Parliament for Finchley

Chapter 5

MEMBER OF PARLIAMENT

Mrs. Thatcher had many political friends in Parliament to help her get acquainted with all the workings of this great democratic institution. The first day she had herself photographed with the policeman who guarded the door. She was now a "backbencher"—one of the members without a particular assignment in the government who therefore sat behind the leadership of her party. "Frontbenchers" was the term used to describe the M.P.'s who were cabinet ministers or had other important assignments in the party. The party not in power, the official opposition (or her majesty's opposition), sat opposite the party in power with its own frontbenchers, spokespeople on the same subjects for which government ministers had responsibilities—the "shadow cabinet." With this seating arrangement, the two major parties faced each other with the leaders on the front row ready to debate issues.

Mrs. Thatcher began at the back, but she made steady progress up the ladder of power. She had no special mentor from among the top people in her party, so her rise cannot be attributed to any special help from this group.

Margaret Thatcher did have a stroke of luck in her very

first term. Because of the amount of legislation introduced by the government, backbenchers had little opportunity to introduce a bill of their own. In order to give everyone a fair chance, at the beginning of the parliamentary session, backbenchers could put their name in for this opportunity to a kind of lottery. Mrs. Thatcher put her name in. While the list that was compiled from the drawing was a long one, only about the first half dozen could expect to be given the time to introduce legislation. With the luck of the draw, Mrs. Thatcher came in second. By chance, first place also went to another new M.P., but of the Labour party.

Now Margaret Thatcher had to hurry up and decide on what legislation to back. At first she thought that she would try a bill on the subject of contempt of court, which had been discussed in a recent court case involving a murdered policeman. However, the attorney general, who was a Conservative, told her that this legislation might be introduced as a government matter. With her deadline approaching, she decided on a bill to admit the press to meetings of local councils. The public had been upset by some of the decisions made by local councils behind closed doors, without the public or the press having access to the discussions by which the decisions were reached. Of course, the press had a strong interest in being able to cover such meetings.

Once her decision had been made, Mrs. Thatcher had to consult experts, gather background material, and draft the legislation. She secured help from the former attorney general and many of the Tory M.P.'s. Her cabinet minister for housing and local government, Henry Brooke, was not enthusiastic about the bill. He wanted a voluntary, not a mandatory, requirement for the admission of the press. However, with the pressure of others from within the Conservative party and the interest of the press in the subject, he agreed that his ministry would give help with the drafting.

Usually early in the session new M.P.'s would give their first speech, which would last only ten to twelve minutes. Mrs. Thatcher had been so busy in the preparations for her bill that she had to forego this opportunity. Her first speech came in the defense of her bill, a much tougher and longer assignment. Bills introduced by individual M.P.'s rather than the government were usually debated on a Friday when many M.P.'s would have already left for the weekends. Because there was so much interest in the subject of her bill, over one hundred members were present to hear her, including all three women members of the government.

Margaret Thatcher spoke for twenty-seven minutes without notes and with a skill that won acclaim. Henry Brooke said:

> She spoke with a fluency which most of us
> would envy. She achieved the rare feat of mak-

ing a Parliamentary reputation on a Friday, a reputation which I am sure she will now proceed to enhance on the earlier days of the week.[1]

The press coverage was good. She seemed to be able to judge the mood of the House in a way exceptional for a newcomer.

Mrs. Thatcher had support from both sides. But there was some opposition to her bill, both from within her party and from the Labour party. When the vote was taken at this point, it was 152 for the bill to 39 against. Now it went to the standing committee where it was reviewed clause by clause with amendments. It takes a good deal of skill to maneuver a Private Member's Bill through this committee. Mrs. Thatcher relied on the advice of her experienced friends. Compromise and negotiation were required. The bill in its final form gave the public rights it had not had before and stopped certain objectionable practices of the councils. The legislation passed the House of Commons, went through the House of Lords (the other, less powerful, branch of Parliament), and received the Royal Assent (approval by a commission appointed by the queen and acting on her behalf). Mrs. Thatcher had succeeded in getting an important law adopted and had gained political experience and acclaim in the process.

Of course, it was luck that she had the chance to propose a

bill, but in politics taking advantage of such opportunities is very important. Mrs. Thatcher had an enviable record for her first session of Parliament.

In the next session beginning in November 1960, Margaret decided to make the work of the treasury her area of specialization. As a tax lawyer, and with her interest in economics, she had the qualifications to address these issues. She joined in the budget debate in 1961 with a well-argued speech on tax issues.

Harold Macmillan was now the prime minister and the leader of the Conservative party. Mrs. Thatcher had great respect for him. He was someone who could pick out future trends. He was able to express his ideas effectively both in speech and in the written word. In October 1961, Mrs. Thatcher was given an appointment with him. She had lunch with her sister Muriel that day and expressed the hope that she might be asked to propose or second the prime minister's speech on the opening day of Parliament.

Instead Margaret Thatcher was offered a more prestigious assignment. She was given the junior post of parliamentary secretary at the ministry of pensions. This post represented a remarkable promotion after only two years in the House. Since a woman had resigned the position, she may have been chosen as the "token" woman to be visible with the men in leadership roles. She enjoyed her work in this ministry because it combined financial issues with human concerns. She liked the policy work involved. Mrs. Thatcher felt that she learned a great deal from John Boyd-Carpenter, who headed the department and was a good debater. As she served under three different ministers at the head of pensions, she was able to observe how the civil service (the bureaucrats or government officials) tailored their advice according to what they thought the minister would accept.

The Conservative government began to encounter election trouble in early 1962. In order to counter inflation from increasing wages, the government had introduced a measure called the "pay pause," a voluntary restraint on income that the government applied strongly to its public employees. The move was not popular. Then the Labour party pressed an attack on pensions and social security. Instead of the minister of pensions making the reply, Mrs. Thatcher was chosen to do so. Since the government had no plans for raising pensions to cover the cost-of-living increases, the assignment was not an easy one or one that many would want. She argued that concern must be given as well to the persons who had to pay the pensions. It was a good defensive reply backed with figures in support of her argument. The press reported favorably on her effort.

Then a minister at the war office was involved in a scandal about the connections his mistress had with the Russian Embassy. Though Mrs. Thatcher supported Macmillan, she was well aware of the sentiment that he should be replaced.

At the very beginning of the Conservative party conference, Macmillan was struck with an illness and resigned.
The leadership of the party was open, and people began
campaigning for the office. The victorious candidate was Sir
Alec Douglas-Home, called Lord Home, the foreign secretary. As a lord, or peer, he was not eligible for a seat in the
House of Commons where the party leader had to be. He had
to renounce his title, win an election for a seat in the House
of Commons, and prepare to lead his party in the general
election. While he did a remarkable job, and Mrs. Thatcher
thought that if they had had several more months they
might have won, the Conservatives lost to the Labour party
that was now led by Harold Wilson. In Finchley, Mrs.
Thatcher's lead was cut almost in half by a strong challenge
by the Liberal candidate. Still she won with a majority of
8,802 votes.

The education secretary, Margaret Thatcher, speaks before a group at a youth center.

Chapter 6

THE OFFICIAL OPPOSITION AND HER MAJESTY'S GOVERNMENT

Now, Mrs. Thatcher was for the first time a member of the opposition. Different opportunities were available in this role. Mrs. Thatcher was asked to be the shadow minister of pensions. Shadow ministers have to study and be ready to present their party's view of the area of government to which they are assigned.

Meanwhile, there was some dissatisfaction among the Tories about their leadership and the selection process by an inside group. Sir Alec Douglas-Home, who did not want to split the party, set up the formal ballot procedure for election of the leader. There then was pressure for this selection procedure to be used. He decided that party unity would be served best if he resigned. Edward Heath won the election to lead the Conservatives.

Mrs. Thatcher was appointed to follow the actions of the ministry of housing and land. Then she was moved to be the number-two spokesperson in the treasury. Later she was promoted to shadow minister of power, next transport, and finally in October 1968, she became shadow minister of education. While all these moves about a year apart meant a great deal of work getting acquainted with the work of the government, they also gave Mrs. Thatcher a well-rounded education in the problems of different areas. This background was to stand her in good stead when she became a member of the real, not just the shadow, cabinet.

The Labour prime minister, Harold Wilson, called for elections when the timing was calculated to favor his party in March 1966. While he had come into office on a 4-vote majority, this time he won a majority of 97. In Finchley, Mrs. Thatcher's majority of 9,464 was slightly better than in the last election, but her percentage of the vote was about the same.

It was during the period when she was in the opposition that an important honor came to her. Although she was just a newcomer to the shadow cabinet, she was invited to give the annual lecture at the big meeting in 1968 of the Conservative Political Centre, the arm of the party whose purpose was to stimulate creative thought and policy. Mrs. Thatcher chose the title, "What's Wrong with Politics?"

In this speech, she set forth her own political philosophy. She felt the greatest mistake of the past few years was too much government and not enough choice for the private citizen.

But the way to get personal involvement and participation is not for people to take part in

more and more governmental decisions but to
make the government reduce the area of decision
over which it presides and consequently leave the
private citizen to "participate," if that be the
fashionable word, by making more of his own
decisions. What we need now is a far greater
degree of personal responsibility and decision,
far more independence from the government,
and a comparative reduction in the role of
government.[1]

People's enthusiastic support of a political party can be expected only if the party has firm beliefs about what it wants to do.

When Mrs. Thatcher was appointed shadow minister of education, the party leader, Mr. Heath, was appointing someone who was not identified with either the right or the left wing of the party on the issues affecting education. The problem the country faced was the growing number of children of school age at the same time that economic crises were cutting into potential increases for spending on education. Many questions about education were being discussed. At what age should children be allowed to leave school? In order to prevent segregation, should all communities be forced to place all publicly funded schools in one comprehensive system? Should parents still be provided with a choice of sending their children to good grammar schools not closest to home as Mrs. Thatcher's parents had done? It was Mrs. Thatcher's job now to shape the policy of the Conservatives in the field of education for the next election fight.

The platform that was made part of the Tory policy included these provisions. The opportunity for a good education was the right of the child and an investment in the nation's future. In budget planning emphasis should be put on the primary schools as the foundation for later education. Nursery schools should be expanded in order to help poorer children overcome social handicaps. Secondary education should permit different patterns with the local people making the decisions for their area. In order to provide an opportunity for children who were "late bloomers," those who developed their talents at a later age, the type of secondary education to which admission would be granted should not be fixed at the age of eleven. The role of the central government is to see that the local authorities provide an opportunity for children to reach the highest level they are capable of achieving at whatever age their abilities and talents may appear.

The age at which young persons can leave school should be raised to sixteen. Direct grants to schools should be encouraged to provide opportunities for children of academic ability regardless of the income of their parents. Parents should have the freedom to send children to independent schools. The increasing demand for university and college training was recognized. The Tories would institute an inquiry into teacher training and the career structure of teachers in order to attract and retain highly qualified persons. These were some of the planks of the Tory platform that Mrs. Thatcher helped craft.

The June 1970 election results were something of a surprise since the public opinion polls showed the election going to the Labour party, but the Conservatives won with a majority of 30. In Finchley, Mrs. Thatcher had an 11,185 majority with a 2.8 percent increase of the vote in her favor over the last election. She felt that it was the cost-of-living issue that had resulted in the Tory victory.

Now with the Conservatives back in power, Mrs. Thatcher was appointed secretary of state for education and science. Her personal background, an education begun in a local council school and culminating in a science degree from Oxford, qualified her for the job. This cabinet post was important. While she might have preferred to be chancellor of the exchequer with responsibilities for economic policy, she did not have the seniority or the experience in 1970 for this position.

During her term in the education post, some important advances were made in the field. Nevertheless, it was at this time that Mrs. Thatcher became tagged in the press as a hard-line right-winger in the party. This reputation stemmed from her first act, which was to reverse the policy of the Labour government requiring a comprehensive pattern for secondary schools. That would force local communities to do away with independent grammar schools to which parents could send their children instead of to neighborhood schools. In doing so, she was implementing the Conservative campaign pledge. She also was reversing a pet project of the National Union of Teachers.

The party was looking for ways to cut government spending. Mrs. Thatcher had to fight to achieve not just a continuation of the funding of new primary school buildings but an increase. Also there was no postponement of the plan to increase the age at which children could leave school. The result of this decision was larger school enrollments. However, she had to demonstrate that her department would economize. The trade-off was the elimination of the provision of free milk at school for children between eight and eleven years old, an increase in the charges for school meals, and the setting of new fees at some previously free London museums and art galleries. Although the cut of the free milk was to cause Margaret Thatcher political trouble in the future, she felt that she had done her best to protect education since the school milk and meals were not "education" as such. Moreover, she tried to protect the children most vulnerable to such cuts by providing free milk in special schools and for children eight to eleven years old for whom it was medically necessary. While charges for meals were increased, she also increased the limits for parents' income for which free meals were provided. The result was that more children would receive free meals, but those whose parents could pay for meals would not be subsidized.

In order to tackle the quality-of-education issue, Mrs. Thatcher appointed a number of committees to study and make recommendations on questions such as in-service training for teachers, illiteracy, the teaching of reading, and use of the English language. One very hot issue was the report of increasing violence in some of the schools. She certainly did not react in a hard-line, right-wing approach to this one. She sought to establish the facts to see whether violence was actually increasing and then to try to tailor a solution that would meet those incidents. She increased by 25 percent the places the children from local primary schools could attend free in direct-grant schools. The fees paid by the parents of the other children in these schools were set by what they could afford. Mrs. Thatcher called these schools a "bridge" between a completely independent system and a state system. She laid future plans for free nursery schooling to begin in deprived areas. She envisioned a plan in which education would begin at an earlier age for more children and the children would have an opportunity to continue it longer.

The attacks from the Labour party shadow cabinet were severe. The previous Labour policy in education had been not just for equality of opportunity but for equality of what was given. Ability was not to enter into the decision of the education to be provided. Talented students were to be educated the same as the untalented. Moreover, the opposition printed up posters with the slogan: "Margaret Thatcher, Milk Snatcher." Some in her own party were arguing that she should be shifted to a new assignment. The personal attack on her only made her more determined to stick with it. Perhaps her reward was to see the Labour party three years later when back in power decide not to restore the free milk because there was no evidence of any bad effect on children's health.

Mrs. Thatcher was heckled by minorities of left-wing students about the school milk issue in June 1971 at the Liverpool Polytechnic and had to leave by a side door. Then, in a move that has been criticized as a political mistake, she raised the issue of the need for reform of some of the uses to which student union funds were being put at the universities. Although students had to pay into the fund, some of the money was being used to pay court fines and contributions to African freedom movements. Mrs. Thatcher suggested that the universities or polytechnic authorities might take over the responsibility of financing student unions. This idea triggered student protests and was opposed by university faculty, so she shelved it. However, she was sorry that she had not been able to get reforms to cover not only the financing of student unions but also some system of democratic voting procedure over the spending of funds so that they would not be controlled by a militant minority.

Meanwhile the Conservative party was headed for economic and political problems. In order to control inflation and increasing unemployment, the government announced that it would take statutory powers to control increases in pay, prices, dividends, and rents. This shift in Tory policy, called Heath's U-turn, did not win the confidence of the people. As a cabinet decision, Mrs. Thatcher was willing to shoulder her share of the responsibility for it. However, since cabinet deliberations are confidential, it is not known the extent to which she supported the shift. The new approach was not consistent with the policy ideas she announced in her earlier speech. Also she was known for being able to challenge ideas in cabinet meetings. Still, the changes were not directly involved with her education department where she was in the midst of controversy and was formulating policy issues relating to her subject.

The unions opposed the Heath policies. With the coal miners on strike and other unions engaging in a work slowdown to protest the wages the government was offering, Heath announced a three-day workweek to save fuel and power. The Middle East countries had cut oil supplies to countries like Britain. Heath called for an election on February 18 to get the voters' approval to deal with the oil crisis. Most of the Conservatives campaigned on the need to control the power of the unions.

While the Conservatives won 300,000 more votes than Labour, Labour won five more seats in the House; yet it was some thirty-two seats behind all the other parties combined. With no clear-cut answer from the voters, it was possible for the Tories to work out a coalition with another party to remain in power. Heath was authorized to discuss the possibility with the leader of the Liberal party. The offer was turned down by the Liberals, and Heath resigned as prime minister. Harold Wilson was again the prime minister and the Labour party formed the government. Mrs. Thatcher had won her election in Finchley with a majority of 5,987, with a smaller constituency because of changed boundaries for the district. She was once again in the opposition.

This time Margaret Thatcher was asked to be the shadow environment minister and to develop a housing policy that would win back some of the voters who owned houses and had turned to the Liberal party since they felt the Conservatives had abandoned their interests. She focused on providing protection for home owners against rising mortgage interest rates. This effort would bring some hope to couples who wanted to work to buy their own homes. Also she wanted persons renting from local government councils to have a chance to buy their homes. By July she had a comprehensive housing plan that was designed to increase greatly the number of people owning homes. Still she had to sell her ideas in her own party. Some wondered whether it was wise to offer subsidies to any group of people when the economic situation was so poor. Also they complained that when other departments had to cut back, she seemed able to win increases—for education in 1970 and now for housing. Finally the party agreed to her plan, but it was to be implemented toward the end of a five-year term so that the details could be planned.

The Labour party dubbed her proposal "Margaret's Midsummer Madness." The Labour plan was to take all property into public ownership. They realized that the Tory proposal might well have more appeal. Mrs. Thatcher claimed that the cost of reducing the mortgage rates could easily be met by stopping the allocations by the government to local councils to buy up private homes.

Wilson called for another election in October to try to strengthen his majority. Mrs. Thatcher was called to give press conferences on the housing issue. When she was challenged as to whether she would be willing to compromise on that policy if after the election it was necessary for the Conservative party to form a coalition with the Liberals, she responded: "No, my policies are *not negotiable*."[2] Many have pointed to this reply as the first indication that she would break with Heath if in a coalition the Liberals forced a compromise. It would mean that she could no longer accept a cabinet position. However, the possibility did not occur because Labour won 319 seats to the Conservatives' 276 and after adding in the votes of the other parties, had a majority of 3. Mrs. Thatcher won a majority of 3,911 but gained a larger share of the vote.

The election had meant not only a loss of seats for the Conservatives, but also a weakening of support in the big towns and cities. With his second election loss, Heath was advised by some of his friends to resign immediately. But he declined to follow this advice.

Instead, he lost the election for the leadership of his party to the challenge by Margaret Thatcher, who then went on to vanquish several other contenders for this position. She was now the head of the Conservative party and the leader of the opposition in the House of Commons.

Margaret Roberts (above) takes a shopping tour and relaxes in a pub (below left) of the Dartford district where she ran as a Conservative candidate, the youngest candidate in the general election of 1950. After she was graduated from Oxford, Margaret began working as a research chemist (below right).

Margaret and Denis Thatcher (above) were married in December 1951 and two years later Carol Jane and Mark (below left) were born. Mark and Carol with their mother in 1961 (below right)

Margaret Thatcher enjoys cooking and having dinner parties in her home (left). In 1971 she visits with some schoolchildren (below).

William Whitelaw, who was running against Margaret in an election, was challenged to give Mrs. Thatcher a kiss and he did (above). After Margaret Thatcher was elected Conservative party leader in March 1979, she is guided from the House of Commons by her campaign manager, Airey Neave (below).

Mr. And Mrs. Denis Thatcher at the wedding of their son, Mark, to Diane Burgdorf (above). Carol Thatcher (left) in 1987

Above: Mrs. Thatcher holds up a cake that represents the key to Number 10 Downing Street. Below: In 1987, supporters of Mrs. Thatcher celebrate at Wembley Arena in London.

Prime Minister Thatcher and President Mikhail Gorbachev of the Soviet Union (left) hold talks in the Kremlin in Moscow. Great Britain's prime minister (below) attends an economic summit with leaders from Canada, England, France, Japan, Italy, the United States, and West Germany in 1988.

Margaret and Denis Thatcher attend the funeral of Airey Neave, who was killed when a terrorist bomb went off in his car.

Chapter 7

LEADER OF THE OPPOSITION

Even though Margaret Thatcher was now leader of the Conservatives, her position was by no means secure. Her 146-vote victory surprised almost everyone. Most of the people that voted for her in 1975 were really voting against Heath. Perhaps two-thirds of them would have preferred someone else if the circumstances had been different. She, herself, was inexperienced. She had not been in the top tier of cabinet officers and part of the ruling group in the party. She had not been asked to become expert in some of the economic and foreign policy issues. She was aware of her weakness, and so while she spoke out boldly, she acted with a good deal of caution.

Mrs. Thatcher did have certain things going in her favor. Not the least was that Ted Heath declined to join her shadow cabinet. One account of her offer of a position is as follows:

Margaret Thatcher began by explaining that she wanted Edward Heath to continue to serve with her.

"Shan't," came the discouraging answer.

Undeterred, she started to ask him to indicate what part he was not willing to take.

"Won't," he cut in.

"What can I say?" she said to him.

"There is nothing to say," he replied.[1]

After a few minutes of silence, she left the room of his home. Rather than face the press waiting outside after she had just entered his house five minutes before, she spoke for fifteen minutes with Heath's private secretary and then left with a "no comment" to the reporters. While it was embarrassing to have Heath hostile toward her whenever they met in public, it was probably better not to have him causing trouble in the shadow cabinet.

The man who represented the Heath wing of the party was William Whitelaw. He was not a good speaker or debater in the cabinet. However, he was a shrewd politician and had a good-natured personality. Instead of fighting Mrs. Thatcher, he was willing to work with her.

Surprisingly, some have felt that one of Mrs. Thatcher's advantages was the fact that she was a woman. She had a great deal of experience dealing with male politicians, but they had little experience in dealing with women politicians.

Moreover, Margaret Thatcher was not a woman of the aristocratic classes, used to deferring to men. As the daughter of a small-town grocer who had achieved her position not because of her connections but because of her talent, she was used to speaking her mind and disagreeing with those whose opinions she could not accept. Many of her colleagues found her style abrasive.

While she had admirers who had helped her win the election for party leader, Mrs. Thatcher was careful to start out with many of the old leaders in her shadow cabinet. She moved to restore unity. On the surface, not much appeared to change during her first eight months in office.

How she performed at the party conference in October was important in predicting how strong she would be. Heath and Whitelaw snubbed her. She won a big ovation after her leader's speech on the final day of the conference. She knew how to appeal to the people. When she spoke about immigration, trade unions, and government spending, she was talking about the fears and concerns of the voters. She knew that the taxpayers wanted to have more of their earnings to spend for themselves. She recognized the need for the Conservative party to practice the "politics of persuasion." Trying to arrange solutions for people as the government had done in the past was not as effective as people doing things for themselves.

Margaret Thatcher felt that:

> You can present people with ideas they may come to believe in, and as a result of them they will act, if they have the opportunities. Presenting people with opportunities is part of what politics is about.[2]

The political and economic situation in Britain was to change radically in the next three and a half years before the 1979 election. Runaway inflation meant that prices had doubled between the beginning of 1974 and the end of 1978. The Labour government was not willing to cut government spending and impose wage controls because such moves would harm their supporters in the trade union movement. The money policies that were put in place to keep full employment were not working. Industrial production declined, and people were unemployed. The Labour party worked with the unions to try to keep wage demands low in order to stimulate industrial growth. Although this move did help to reduce inflationary growth some, by March 1976, much to everyone's surprise, Harold Wilson, the Labour prime minister, resigned. He was replaced by James Callaghan. It was Callaghan who had to cut government spending (a policy later to be associated with Thatcher) in order to obtain financial backing from the International Monetary Fund.

Mrs. Thatcher spotted this issue as one that the Conservatives could use. The Tories went to work to prepare an economic policy statement for the next election. Mrs. Thatcher became convinced that the Labour party was leading Britain into socialism and that the Conservatives, by trying to occupy the middle ground, were unwittingly helping them. As she remarked to a colleague: "Standing in the middle of the road is very dangerous, you get knocked down by the traffic from both sides."[3]

While the Labour party was having its trouble in dealing with the economy, the Tories were not presenting a united front. At the 1978 party conference, Heath spoke in favor of a wage-control policy even though the Labour party plan did not seem to be working. Thatcher in her leader's speech at the end of the conference gave unqualified support to free collective bargaining when the Conservatives came to power. The applause for her position made it clear that the party faithful backed her position. She tried, however, not to accentuate the differences between herself and Heath in her public statements.

In the winter of 1978-79 that became known as the Winter of Discontent, Britain was plagued by strikes of public workers that crippled normal living. Garbage was not collected. Children had to be kept home from school because of the strike of school workers. Grave diggers would not work. Sick people were kept from hospitals. There was violence on picket lines. The unions for government workers lost the sympathy of the public. While Callaghan made light of the crisis, Mrs. Thatcher took advantage of public opinion to call for support for curbs on the powers of the unions. She had proposals for reform—some of which may have gone beyond the wishes of her own shadow cabinet members.

The Labour party, in order to stop the strikes, had to undermine its wage-control policy by granting increases to public-sector workers that were twice the policy limit. With this increase, other workers were dissatisfied with their pay. The unions could no longer control their members. The cooperation between unions and the Labour party broke down.

In January Callaghan had twice succeeded in defending against votes that would bring the government down and force an election. Each challenge brought narrower margins for him. Then in March Mrs. Thatcher called for a vote of No Confidence.

The opposition party can do this, and if there is a vote in favor, the government must resign. Since the party in power can usually get all its members to vote with the party, ordinarily the motion fails, and the government remains in power.

Not since 1924 had a prime minister been ousted in this way. However, there was discontent in the Labour party. The vote was taken, and the motion carried by 311 votes to 310. The Conservatives cheered. Whitelaw put his arm around Margaret Thatcher and congratulated her. When she returned home, she told her husband it had been "exciting. A night like this comes once in a lifetime."[4]

Her joy was to be cut short two days later by a bomb that killed Airey Neave, the man who had managed her campaign for leadership of the Conservatives. He had been shadow secretary of state for Northern Ireland and was killed. A bomb that was attached to his car in the House of Commons parking lot by the Irish National Liberation Army exploded. The centuries-long conflict between the Irish and the British was now centered on a fight over control of Northern Ireland, but the bombs set by the Irish National Liberation Army have often been placed in and around London. To have a terrorist bomb set to kill an M.P. near Parliament was shocking.

Mrs. Thatcher had been attending a children's festival in Finchley and did not hear the news until she returned to London to do a broadcast. She went to the House of Commons where she wrote a tribute for Neave. She called on his widow, Diane, and offered her a position working on the election campaign that was to take place because the Conservatives won the vote of No Confidence in the House. It was a thoughtful gesture that was characteristic of Margaret Thatcher.

The election campaign was a strenuous one with Mrs. Thatcher outpacing all her staff. She seemed to thrive on the work. The Labour party set out to portray her as the right-wing extremist who would tear up all the Labour programs. The Tories countered: "This election is about the future of Britain—a great country which seems to have lost its way."[5] Neither candidate wanted the fight to look bitter. Callaghan did not want to be seen as a man out to beat a woman. Thatcher did not want to appear as a shrill female. Indeed she received advice from the director of publicity for the Conservative party, Gordon Reece, about lowering her voice, speaking more slowly, softening her hairstyle, and smiling more.

She followed this advice but refused other suggestions to soften her attacks on the unions and to include Heath in the spotlight. She waged a successful national campaign, but she had to pay attention to Finchley too. If she wasn't elected to her seat in the House of Commons, she could not be prime minister. On election day, May 3, she was at the polls in Finchley greeting the voters.

Waiting for the election results was not easy. The early national returns were not too promising. Mrs. Thatcher was aware that if the Conservatives did not win, she would be replaced quickly as leader of the party. As the evening progressed, the results began to look better. After her own election was secure with a majority of 7,900 votes, she drove with her husband to the Conservative central office. They arrived at 3:00 A.M. and were greeted by a roar from the crowds gathered in the square outside. The result continued to be favorable. Champagne was opened, but she drank little. She asked her publicity director if he had thought of an appropriate statement for her to make when she went to Number 10 Downing Street, the official residence of the prime ministers. He replied that he had, and the two went into another room. He read her words adapted from the prayer of St. Francis of Assisi: "Where there is discord may we bring harmony, where there is error may we bring truth, where there is doubt may we bring faith, and where there is despair may we bring hope."

Mrs. Thatcher's eyes filled with tears for the first time that day.

The Conservatives had won 339 seats, a net gain of 55, with a majority in the House of 43. Margaret Thatcher was to be the next prime minister of Great Britain.

Prime Minister Margaret Thatcher and her husband, Denis, in front of their official residence at Number 10 Downing Street

Chapter 8

BEGINNING AS PRIME MINISTER

She was not prime minister yet. First, James Callaghan had to go to Buckingham Palace to resign. Then, the queen had to summon Margaret Thatcher to ask her to form a government. Mrs. Thatcher, accompanied by her family, drove to the Conservative central office. Celebrating already had begun. A chocolate cake had been baked in the shape of a number ten, her new address on Downing Street. Across the top of the cake in icing was written: "Margaret Thatcher's Success Story." Mrs. Thatcher thanked her supporters for their hard work. She polished the remarks she would make as she stood outside her new home. Then the family and a few others settled down to wait for the phone call.

The telephone rang. Her assistant answered. It was a wrong number. The telephone rang again. The assistant announced that it was Mr. Heath calling to offer congratulations. Mrs. Thatcher asked that her thanks be conveyed to him. Five more minutes passed, and then the phone rang a third time. It was the queen's secretary calling. Mrs. Thatcher went to the phone in the outer office. Just as everyone was straining to hear the conversation, she closed the door with her foot.

Queen Elizabeth II met her in the study on the first floor of Buckingham Palace. The audience lasted forty-five minutes and went very well. Both women had wondered how they would get along. The relationship got off to a good start. Then accompanied by her husband, who had been waiting with some palace aides, they made their way to their new home. The area at Number 10 Downing Street was jammed with reporters and well-wishers who sang "For She's a Jolly Good Fellow." As she stood on the steps of her new home she quoted the words of St. Francis and then added:

> To all the British people, howsoever they may have voted, may I say this: now that the election is over, may we get together and strive to serve and strengthen the country of which we are so proud to be a part. And, finally, one last thing: in the words of Airey Neave, whom we had hoped to bring here with us, "Now there is work to be done."[1]

Her first work was to select a cabinet. She wanted persons with convictions, willing to work together for a purpose rather than just to get along with others or to adjust to the situation. After her experience with the shadow cabinet, she wanted people who would pull together and not get bogged down with a lot of arguments.

That may have been her wish, but Margaret Thatcher had to be sensitive to the various elements in her party if she wanted to accomplish anything. Some have said that she made a political mistake by not being more ruthless at the beginning in weeding out those who would not agree with her. However, she was effective in working around, if not with, her cabinet. Many were surprised that she did not seek a consensus of views, but she had been very open in her emphasis on her cabinet acting on conviction and going in a clear direction.

Mrs. Thatcher placed her key supporters in positions that controlled economic policy. Her cabinet soon learned that she would get her policy recommendations from the persons she wanted them from, regardless of past tradition. The government's first budget that was submitted a few weeks after she came to power gave a clear signal that she intended to push ahead at once with some of her policies without consulting the cabinet first. She had campaigned on these issues, and the problem of inflation was serious. As she was later to recall about 1979: "We were very near to having what I would call a permanent socialist society where freedom was constantly being diminished."[2]

Mrs. Thatcher is one of the few persons to have an "ism" named after her. "Thatcherism" involves finding the truth about a situation, being evangelical in proclaiming this truth to the people, and discovering the means of applying a solution to the problem. It is not just a set of policies. Mrs. Thatcher believed that a kind of revolution was necessary in order to get Britain out of the economic mess the country was in and to restore freedom to the people.

Just as the cabinet was to learn that she was not going to fit the mold of her predecessors, so also the civil service would be reminded that it was she who had been elected by the people. While she had great respect for individual civil servants, she felt that it was this group of government employees that bogged down action in red tape and refused to consider radical solutions to problems. It was easier for them just to keep on doing what they had always done. Sir John Hokyns, who was head of her policy unit in Downing Street, described her attitude toward the civil service as follows:

> I think first her temperament and background make her impatient with the whole sort of establishment culture and way of thinking, even of talking. And that, I think, is extremely healthy because I happen to think the Establishment . . . is absolutely at the heart of the British disease. She's gone further than that because she has been prepared to be extremely unreasonable in order to get change—impossible on occasions and many people of a more

gentlemanly and old-fashioned upbringing were rather shocked at the way she carried on.[3]

When the treasury department did not come up with the government expense cuts she needed and when she was told that it could not be done, Mrs. Thatcher called ten of the treasury leaders to her office and gave them a dressing down. In one week she had 1,400 million pounds in cuts.

The international community was soon to discover that there was a new-style British prime minister in office. When Margaret Thatcher went to the European Economic Community summit in Dublin, Ireland, she was well aware of the fact that the EEC was not helping Britain economically. Britain was paying 800 million pounds into the EEC's annual budget and that was more than the country was receiving from the EEC. She refused to accept a compromise and was not conciliatory or diplomatic. After further meetings, she won what she wanted for Britain.

Yet she was open to new ideas and could be persuaded to change her mind. In the creation of the independent nation of Zimbabwe, Mrs. Thatcher started out with one viewpoint, but changed it to support the new constitution based on democratic elections and a parliamentary democracy. When it looked as though the leader of a Marxist party would win, she was under pressure to change again. However, she held firm to the principle of free elections. If the Marxist leader was elected (as he was), Britain should remain true to its commitment. Britain was praised by the international community for its stand.

Throughout 1980, Mrs. Thatcher's ratings in the opinion polls were dropping because of the difficult economic situation at home. Unemployment was high. Industrial bankruptcies were at a record level. Criticism came from many directions. She was urged to spend her way out of the recession. Her supporters acknowledged that the times were tough, but her economic policies needed time to bring results. When she went to the October 1980 Conservative party conference, she told her backers that she would not make turns in policy—referring to Heath's U-turn in 1972—when she knew it was wrong. Margaret Thatcher received a six-minute standing ovation.

The Conservatives now experimented with a new policy to reach their goal of curbing inflation. They decided to cut interest rates and cut public spending in order to stimulate the growth of the private sector economy (that sector not controlled by the government). The 1981 budget was the most radical anti-inflationary one yet, at the very time the economy was down. People were shocked because it was a break with some of the current economic theories.

There was opposition within Mrs. Thatcher's cabinet, but there was not much that cabinet members could do without giving power to the Labour party. Inner-city riots that broke out in London, Liverpool, Manchester, and Bristol showed the extent of public discontent with the economy.

In order to get the government spending cuts she needed, Margaret Thatcher had to get the cooperation of all departments in her cabinet or she had to change some of the members of her cabinet. Since she could not get cooperation from all, a change in the cabinet was necessary. When she made it, it was a sweeping change.

She proceeded to make reforms in trade union law by giving more power back to the union members. Mrs. Thatcher correctly assessed the wishes of her voters. Indeed, one of the significant aspects of her elections has been the working-class support she has received.

The year 1981 was a turning point for Mrs. Thatcher. It took a great deal of courage to weather the bad economic times and the controversy of 1980 and 1981, but toward the end of 1981 some good news appeared. Inflation began to fall and continued to do so for the next eighteen months. Productivity figures for 1981 were the best since the war. There were fewer strikes than at any time since 1939. Still unemployment was over three million. While the Conservatives had recovered in the opinion polls somewhat, they were just even with Labour and Liberals. It was in this situation that a radical change was in the offing.

Also, it was at this time in January 1982 that Mrs. Thatcher faced a personal crisis. Her son, Mark, had been taking part in a car race, the Paris to Dakar rally, and was lost in the Sahara. He was reported missing at a checkpoint in the race. Then word came that he had been found and rescued by helicopter. Then that news was corrected to report that he was still missing. Mrs. Thatcher had to carry on with her work, but it cannot have been easy. When a reporter told her that there was still no news of Mark as she was entering a hotel to give a speech, she broke down and sobbed. However, she composed herself and gave a twenty-five-minute speech. Her husband flew out to the Sahara to get firsthand reports of the search. When she learned that her son was safe six days after the first report of his missing, she went right back to work. It is reported that Mark on his return home was welcomed back, but also given a lecture about the trouble he had caused to both Algeria and Britain with the search efforts.

Her next crisis was to be of an entirely different dimension. On April 2, 1982, the Argentines invaded the Falkland Islands claimed by Britain.

Chapter 9

LEADER DURING THE FALKLANDS WAR

The Falklands comprise two large and about two hundred small islands in the South Atlantic about eight thousand miles from Britain. They have been a British territory for about 150 years, and the people who live there want to remain British. The islands are no great prize: the greatest commercial operation is raising sheep.

The Argentines had disputed the British claim. A new military regime in Argentina, headed by General Leopoldo Galtieri, wanted to win popular favor in his country and unify his nation by challenging the British to give back this territory.

Some former British governments had given some thought to doing just that because the islands were so hard to defend at that distance. However, the eighteen hundred English-speaking inhabitants of the islands were mostly of British origin. They did not want to be Argentines.

The Argentines believed that the British would never fight to defend the islands. Once leader of the world, Britain was now viewed by some as a third-rate nation in decline. Even when warned by the United States secretary of state, Alexander Haig, that the British would fight and win and that the United States would support Britain, the Argentines responded that Britain would never fight.

The British also believed that the Argentines would never fight for the islands. In 1976, when some Argentine technicians landed on one of the islands, a mild diplomatic protest was enough to take care of the problem. The foreign office had even considered a land lease-back arrangement with the Argentines, but the Falklands lobby, a group of M.P.'s mainly from the right wing of the Conservative party, opposed any dilution of British sovereignty. When Mrs. Thatcher was told about the lease-back plan, she opposed it. When, in spite of Mrs. Thatcher's objections, the cabinet minister brought up the plan in Parliament, he was attacked. Finally the foreign secretary had to step in and assure the members that nothing would be done against the wishes of the islanders.

An armed British ice patrol boat, the HMS *Endurance*, was stationed in the Falklands. It was withdrawn to cut military expenses. However, this action sent the wrong message to the Argentines. Also, the British Nationality Bill was adopted, which dealt with the larger issue of who was a British national but which had the effect of depriving about eight hundred of the islanders of British citizenship. February intelligence information reported an increase in Argentine military activity in the South Atlantic. On March 20, an Argentine scrap-metal merchant raised his nation's flag on one of the islands and was forced to leave by a unit of the Royal Marines from the *Endurance*, which had not yet sailed from the Falklands. On March 28, Mrs. Thatcher ordered three nuclear submarines to the South Atlantic. The Argentine fleet started sailing toward the islands on March 31, and their forces landed on April 2.

When it was learned that the Argentine fleet was on its way to the Falklands, Britain's foreign secretary and the minister of defense were in foreign countries. Mrs. Thatcher called other senior officials for a conference. The possibility of mounting a defense presented many difficulties. After the meeting had been going for a time without any successful strategy proposal, Admiral Sir Henry Leach, the first sea lord and chief of naval staff, arrived. He presented a positive plan of action to send a task force to recapture the islands. It was important to Mrs. Thatcher to be able to take action because without it, if the Falklands were lost, she would have to resign. It was important to Admiral Leach to demonstrate the effectiveness of the navy in order to prevent military spending cuts from wiping out his surface fleet.

Preparations were begun immediately. Argentina invaded the Falklands Friday morning, April 2. The day after, Mrs. Thatcher faced an angry emergency session of Parliament. Not since Britain's involvement in the Suez crisis in 1956 had the House met on a Saturday. She was able to announce that the task force would be sent that weekend.

One of the first casualties of the war was the foreign secretary who, with his team, resigned in the face of criticism that the foreign office was controlled by appeasers who would rather talk than fight. Mrs. Thatcher tried to persuade him to remain in office because she had confidence in him, but she deferred to his decision and recognized that some changes would have to be made in the cabinet if the government were to survive.

Mrs. Thatcher appealed for support from the world community on the basis that Britain was defending the principle of self-determination—the right of a people to decide their own government. In the face of this argument, even the Organization of American States that might have been expected to side with Argentina did not support its own member. At the United Nations, Resolution 502, calling for the withdrawal of Argentine forces, was adopted by the Security Council with the Soviet Union abstaining. To the United States Mrs. Thatcher cast the conflict as a test of Western resolve to fight aggression, which if not met would have devastating consequences for the Western democracies. She won the backing of the United States. Whereas during the Suez crisis, Britain had isolated herself and been condemned by the world community, in the Falklands War Britain marshaled world opinion in her favor. In this achievement, Mrs. Thatcher's emphasis on principle and her personal diplomacy played a major role.

How did she respond to her duties as a wartime leader? From the time of the Argentine invasion, Margaret Thatcher realized that Britain would have to fight. She was worried. The casualty figures that came in were a burden to her. William Whitelaw, who had commanded troops in World War II, took her aside and counseled her that she could not show signs of doubt because then the officers in her armed forces might not be so willing to commit their troops, with the result that even more lives could be lost. She was given this praise by the chief of the defense staff, Admiral Sir Terence Lewin:

> She was a decisive leader, which is what of course the military want. We don't want somebody who vacillates, we want to be able to put the case to her, the requirements to her, and say this is how it is, this is the decision we want, we want it now and we want it quickly and we don't want a wishy-washy decision, we want a clear-cut decision. She was magnificent in her support of the military.[1]

Although she was firm in her resolve in a way that her new foreign secretary often was not, Mrs. Thatcher also was willing to attempt a negotiated peace before unconditional surrender. She was effective in gauging the mood of the

British and relating to it as she made speeches during the time that the casualty figures were coming in. She wore dark colors during the period of the hostilities and showed her concern in a way that won the support of the country. When the Argentines finally surrendered on June 14, she greeted the news with one word, "Rejoice!" It was a release for her from the anxiety and responsibility with which she had lived. She felt that no problem she could face as prime minister could top the Falklands crisis.

The victory did wonders for the morale and the pride of the British. The country had worked together during the war and been united by a common purpose. Mrs. Thatcher's popularity was as high as at any time since she took office. Still there was criticism of her and her government. A special committee was appointed to study the Falklands crisis to determine whether the government could have foreseen the Argentine invasion and whether it could have done anything to prevent the invasion.

The committee that was composed of members from both the Labour and Conservative parties and a distinguished civil servant reported that the invasion could not have been foreseen. The question of prevention was more complex. Even if the government had taken other courses of action that were examined, there was no reasonable basis for the suggestion that the invasion could be prevented. Dr. David Owen, Labour foreign secretary from 1977 to 1979, gave this assessment of Margaret Thatcher's conduct:

> She knew she was playing for enormous stakes. But once she accepted them, she behaved outstandingly well. Some potential Prime Ministers might have accepted the invasion, decided not to throw the Argentine out, and worked out some compromise. I have never doubted that such a course would have been absolutely devastating for this country. Mrs. Thatcher recognized that from the start, instinctively, and deserves credit for it.[2]

Prime Minister Thatcher arrives home at Number 10 Downing Street after a five-day tour of the Falkland Islands.

Chapter 10

GETTING REELECTED

The Falklands War did much to strengthen Mrs. Thatcher's reputation as an international leader. She was seen as the friend, but also the friendly critic, of the United States. Her hand was strengthened in negotiations with European nations.

At home there was still criticism of her economic policies and the failure to solve the unemployment problem. Industrial production was low. Pressure for nuclear disarmament was building. There was uncertainty about when Mrs. Thatcher would ask for the next elections to be held. She decided that this uncertainty was having a bad effect on the economy, so she set the date of June 9, 1983, as the date of the next election.

The main Labour platform promised government spending on public works to reduce unemployment, taking Britain out of the European Economic Community, working for a non-nuclear defense policy, and closing down independent schools. The Conservatives promised trade union legislation and privatization of certain industries (that is, offering stock for industries the government owned). Labour attacks on Mrs. Thatcher for her role in the war backfired.

In her own party several times she found it necessary to correct her new foreign secretary, Francis Pym—once when he suggested that the sovereignty of the Falklands was negotiable, and once when he suggested that too many votes for the Conservatives might not be good for the government. On the latter issue, she said that she thought that she could handle a landslide all right.

Her opponents were divided on important issues, and it was said that their failure to agree lost them the election. While it looked very doubtful at the beginning of the year that Mrs. Thatcher could win the election, by June her victory was predictable. She won 397 seats, giving her a 144 majority over all the other parties put together. It was the largest number of seats controlled since World War II. She was the first Conservative prime minister in the twentieth century to win a second consecutive term. It is said that she was the strongest Conservative prime minister for a hundred years. The gamble to make Margaret Thatcher leader of the Conservatives appeared to have paid off.

When she reshuffled her cabinet, the foreign secretary, Francis Pym, whom she had to correct during the campaign, was out. As a skilled parliamentarian, he knew how to start a rebellion against her. In May of 1985, when economic conditions were not good, he tried to do just that by establishing a new group of Conservatives in what he perceived to be a more central position to unite all parts of the country. The movement lasted only one weekend. Other Tories made it known that assistance to Pym's group would not be forgiven. However, the attempt shows that Mrs. Thatcher's position was not above challenge.

Opposition also came from Arthur Scargill, president of the National Union of Mineworkers, who called for a political strike to bring down the government—not one for wages or working conditions. Since he was not able to get the miners to vote to go out on strike, he engineered a strike to begin in 1984 with his own pickets. The secret service later estimated that the Soviets contributed seven million pounds to this cause. The government had substantial reserves of coal. Margaret Thatcher appointed Peter Walker as minister for energy because of his skills as a communicator. He would be able to present the government's case best to the television public. The government announced plans to close the uneconomical coal pits.

Many of the miners were opposed to the strike. Large numbers of police were moved in to protect the miners who continued to work from Scargill's pickets. The battles that broke out were fought by police against pickets with Mrs. Thatcher following her policy of noninterference in industrial disputes. The miners in the productive pits were the heroes as far as the Conservatives were concerned because they refused to strike even when subjected to physical and verbal abuse by the pickets. Instead they formed an independent union. Moreover, other unions put off by the violence refused to support Scargill. Union members used legal means to tie up union funds that Scargill was using. By March 1985 so many of the workers had returned to the mines that Scargill had to call off the strike. The right of management to manage and the right of workers to be free to vote to strike had been established.

With the Scargill challenge over, Thatcher had survived the greatest test of her second term. She strongly supported trade unionism, but she wanted to see it as a force in the industrial sphere rather than the Labour party. She emphasized the fact that union members have different political views. The unions themselves began to change by adjusting to new market and technological conditions.

It was in the autumn of 1984 that public sympathy again was strongly mobilized in support of Mrs. Thatcher. The Irish Republican Army bombed the Brighton Conservative party conference with the intention of killing the prime minister and her cabinet. Although several important Tories were killed and others were injured, Mrs. Thatcher was not hurt because she was busy in the early hours of the morning working on her keynote speech in another part of the building. True to form, twelve hours later, she was proclaiming her government's intention to wipe out terrorism wherever it was found.

During Mrs. Thatcher's first term, home ownership rose

in Britain thanks largely to the sale of publicly owned homes to the citizens. During her second term, she went into the business of selling shares of other publicly owned industries. This practice has been followed since by many other countries because it raises funds, eliminates public expense, improves efficiency, and wins votes. It fits well with her goal of a property-owning democracy. Moreover, broad ownership of the industries, especially by employees becoming stockholders, was probably the best guarantee that a future socialist government would have a difficult time renationalizing the companies. Moreover, privatization gave impetus to better management and greater productivity. It contributed to the growth of a class of people whose wealth depends on their enterprise rather than on whom they know or whose votes they control. To Mrs. Thatcher's way of looking at it, she has simply given the "family silver back to the family."[1]

By 1986 with the economy looking brighter, Mrs. Thatcher could propose a budget that permitted spending on projects that would endear her to the voters. She surprised everyone. Social security spending was increased. A tax cut was benefiting the voter by the time of the election on June 11, 1987.

Yet there were many political crises during 1986. There were leaks to the press about a matter that raised questions about Mrs. Thatcher's integrity as a politician. The United States air strike on Colonel Muammar al-Qaddafi in Libya from air bases in Britain was controversial. Mrs. Thatcher saw the American action as a test of the Western alliance's willingness to fight against terrorism. There was opposition to American companies buying up British automobile companies with the fear of the loss of British jobs. Although the government wanted to repeal restrictions on trading on Sunday, the Conservatives themselves voted the bill down.

Commonwealth countries were calling for sanctions against South Africa because of the apartheid policy, but Mrs. Thatcher refused to back sanctions because she felt they were counterproductive and wrong, just as she also felt that apartheid was wrong.

Moreover, she did not see the Commonwealth ties as valuable to Britain in the way that her European and United States connections were. However the queen, who benefits from the Commonwealth ties, was rumored to favor the sanctions. The possible clash did not enhance Mrs. Thatcher's popularity. Finally, the government opposed the publication of a book called *Spycatcher* as a violation of the Official Secrets Act. The government lost a court test, and the book hit the best-seller lists when published.

In spite of all these problems in 1986, the polls of her popularity that had dipped began to recover. The economy was strong. Margaret Thatcher called the next election for June 11, 1987. Before the election, there were her visit to Moscow to meet Mr. Gorbachev and the Western economic summit meeting in Venice, which spotlighted her role as an international leader. It is surprising that Mrs. Thatcher, who was identified as an anti-Communist in the earlier period of détente and who had been tagged "The Iron Lady" by the Russians, should have been treated with such respect by the Russians as was shown in their arrangements for the visit. The relationship between Mrs. Thatcher and Mr. Gorbachev was based on mutual respect. They could be honest with each other and know that neither one would convert the other. In order to influence someone, she said that you start talking with them. She felt that her relationship with the United States was based on the fact that the two countries could have frank discussion and that they trusted each other. The economic summit meeting in Venice gave her a chance to show off her economic advances and advertise the extent that other nations were following Britain's lead. In the eight years since she had become prime minister, Britain's role as a world power had improved dramatically.

While many commentators have felt that the Labour party ran a smoother publicity campaign than the Conservatives, Labour picked up only 20 more seats than in 1983. Mrs. Thatcher was returned to power with a majority of 104 seats in the House of Commons. She has been in office now as prime minister longer than anyone else in modern history.

What lies ahead for the future? The British Conservatives went back to Brighton for their annual conference in October 1988 to make plans for their party into the 1990s. The economy is strong although inflation is creeping up somewhat and is their biggest concern. Mrs. Thatcher has turned her attention to the social agenda. She has a vision for Britain as a "responsible society":

> A responsible society is one in which people do not leave it to the person next door to do the job. It is one in which people help each other, where parents put their children first, friends look out for the neighbours, families for their elderly members, that is the starting point for care and support—the unsung efforts of millions of individuals, the selfless work of thousands upon thousands of volunteers . . . Caring isn't measured by what you say; it's expressed by what you do.[2]

Also she has expressed concern about environmental issues such as the greenhouse effect, the depletion of the ozone layer, and acid rain. She has said that she would like to go for a fourth term and perhaps even a fifth.

Not everyone is a supporter of Mrs. Thatcher. She has been accused of being arrogant. She is criticized for having centralized power. It is said that through her many directives she runs a "nanny" government, referring to persons, usually women, who look after other people's children.

The daughter of the grocer from the town of Grantham, who had to work hard to get into Oxford and to achieve professional and political recognition, has been the leader of a revolution that ended the socialist era and stopped the decline of Great Britain. Here is a current assessment of her achievement:

> Politics is usually about what people want, what they want for themselves and their families, what they want for their society and their country. Mrs. Thatcher has excited expectations of a certain kind. She had taught more people to want to own their homes, to want to own a stake in things, to want a better chance for their children. To demean these as "materialist," or even "selfish," is to fail to understand the equality and freedom which material prosperity confers. But even with that important proviso "Thatcherism" has been about something more than material advancement. She, more powerfully than anyone else, has articulated the moral doubts and yearnings of her age. For what people wanted, surely, was an end to decline, release from the corrosive sense of failure, a government which governed, and a

country to begin to be proud of once again. The future may not be hers but she has set its agenda.[3]

NOTES

Chapter 1
1. George Gardiner, *Margaret Thatcher: From Childhood to Leadership* (London: William Kimber, 1975): 174.
2. Russell Lewis, *Margaret Thatcher: A Personal and Political Biography* (London: Routledge & Kegan Paul, Rev. ed. 1984): 104.
3. Gardiner, *Margaret Thatcher: From Childhood to Leadership*, 224.
4. Ibid., 184.
5. Ibid., 226.
6. Ibid., 195.
7. Ibid., 196.
8. Ibid., 203.
9. Ibid., 203.
10. "A Tough Lady for the Tories," *Time* (February 24, 1975): 31.

Chapter 2
1. Gardiner, *Margaret Thatcher: From Childhood to Leadership*, 1.

Chapter 3
1. Nicholas Wapshott & George Brock, *Thatcher* (London: Macdonald & Co., 1983): 43.
2. Gardiner, *Margaret Thatcher: From Childhood to Leadership*, 37.
3. Ibid., 41.
4. Wapshott & Brock, *Thatcher*, 41.

Chapter 4
1. Gardiner, *Margaret Thatcher: From Childhood to Leadership*, 50.
2. Ibid., 52.

Chapter 5
1. Gardiner, *Margaret Thatcher: From Childhood to Leadership*, 64-65.

Chapter 6
1. Gardiner, *Margaret Thatcher: From Childhood to Leadership*, 210.
2. Ibid., 160.

Chapter 7
1. Ernle Money, *Margaret Thatcher-First Lady of the House* (London: Leslie Frewin, 1975): 95.
2. Kenneth Harris, *Thatcher* (Boston: Little, Brown, 1988): 61-62.
3. Harris, *Thatcher*, 69.
4. Penny Junor, *Margaret Thatcher: Wife, Mother, Politician* (London: Sidwidk & Jackson, 1983): 122.
5. Junor, *Margaret Thatcher: Wife, Mother, Politician*, 124.

Chapter 8
1. Junor, *Margaret Thatcher: Wife, Mother, Politician*, 131.
2. Harris, *Thatcher*, 91.
3. Ibid., 95.

Chapter 9
1. Harris, *Thatcher*, 136.
2. Ibid., 144.

Chapter 10
1. Harris, *Thatcher*, 189.
2. Ibid., 219.
3. Peter Jenkins, *Mrs. Thatcher's Revolution* (Cambridge, MA: Harvard University Press, 1988): 379.

Margaret Thatcher 1925-

1925 Margaret Roberts is born, October 13. Unemployment Insurance Act is enacted in Britain. Hitler reorganizes Nazi party and publishes volume one of *Mein Kampf*.

1926 Queen Elizabeth II is born. Germany is admitted to the League of Nations.

1928 Women's suffrage in Britain is reduced from the age of 30 to 21. Herbert Hoover is elected president of the U.S.

1929 Ramsey MacDonald forms Labour government in Britain. Black Friday in New York; the U.S. Stock Exchange collapses and starts the Great Depression.

1930 In the German election, Nazis gain 107 seats from the center parties.

1932 Franklin D. Roosevelt is elected president of the U.S. in a landslide.

1933 Adolf Hitler is appointed chancellor of Germany. Political parties, other than the Nazis, are suppressed. Approximately 60,000 artists (authors, actors, painters, musicians) emigrate from Germany.

1934 Hitler and Benito Mussolini of Italy meet in Venice. German plebescite votes for Hitler as führer. Winston Churchill warns British Parliament of German air menace.

1936 King George V of England dies; he is succeeded by his son Edward VIII. Gossip begins in London about King Edward VIII's relationship with Mrs. Wallis Simpson. He abdicates and is succeeded by his brother, George VI. Mussolini and Hitler proclaim the Rome-Berlin Axis.

1937 George VI is crowned king of Great Britain. Edward, now the Duke of Windsor, marries Wallis Simpson.

1938 Germany mobilizes. Neville Chamberlain meets Hitler. Churchill leads public outcry at British appeasement. Roosevelt recalls U.S. ambassador to Germany.

1939 Germany concludes nonaggression pact with U.S.S.R. and alliance with Italy. King George VI and Queen Elizabeth visit the U.S. Germany invades Poland and annexes Danzig. Great Britain and France declare war on Germany. Roosevelt declares U.S. neutral.

1940 Rationing begins in England. Germany invades Norway and Denmark. Churchill makes "blood, sweat, and tears" speech. Heavy air raids rain on London. U.S. passes Selective Service Act to mobilize the military. Roosevelt elected president of the U.S. for third term.

1941 Germany invades the Soviet Union. Churchill and Roosevelt meet and sign Atlantic Charter. Royal Air Force bombs Nuremberg, Germany. Japanese bomb Pearl Harbor. U.S. and Britain declare war on Japan. Germany and Italy declare war on U.S. U.S. declares war on Germany and Italy.

1942 Germans reach Stalingrad, U.S.S.R. The murder by the Nazis of millions of Jews in gas chambers begins.

1943 Margaret Roberts begins her studies at Oxford University. New German attacks on London. Allied forces in North Africa are placed under General Dwight Eisenhower's command. U.S. forces regain islands in Pacific from Japanese. Churchill, Roosevelt, and Joseph Stalin of the U.S.S.R. hold Teheran Conference. Allied "round-the-clock" bombing of Germany begins.

1944 Heavy air raids on London. D-day: Allies land on Normandy. General Charles DeGaulle enters Paris. U.S. troops land in the Philippines. Roosevelt elected for fourth term.

1945 Roosevelt dies and Harry Truman becomes president of U.S. Mussolini is killed by Italian partisans. Hitler commits suicide. Berlin surrenders to Soviets and Germany capitulates. V.E. Day ends war in Europe. Churchill, Truman, and Stalin confer at Potsdam. General election in Britain brings Labour landslide. Clement Atlee becomes prime minister. U.S. drops atomic bombs on Hiroshima and Nagasaki. Japan surrenders.

1946 United Nations General Assembly holds its first session in London.

1948 Margaret Roberts attends Conservative party conference as representative of the Oxford graduates.

1950 Margaret Roberts is defeated in her first campaign for membership in Parliament.

1951 Margaret Roberts and Denis Thatcher are wed.

1952 King George VI dies; he is succeeded by his daughter Queen Elizabeth II. Churchill announces that Britain has produced an atomic bomb. Eisenhower is elected president of the U.S.

1953 Margaret Thatcher gives birth to twins. Queen Elizabeth II is crowned.

1954 Margaret Thatcher becomes qualified to practice law.

1955 Churchill resigns; succeeded by Anthony Eden.

1957 Anthony Eden resigns as prime minister of Great Britain.

1958 Margaret Thatcher becomes a member of Parliament. European Common Market comes into being.

1960 Margaret Thatcher plays active role in Parliament on tax issues. John F. Kennedy is elected president of the U.S.

1961 Mrs. Thatcher given the junior post of parliamentary secretary at the ministry of pensions. Edward Heath begins negotiations for British entry into Common Market.

1963 Harold Wilson becomes leader of British Labour party. President John F. Kennedy assassinated; Lyndon B. Johnson becomes president.

1964 Harold Wilson becomes the British prime minister.

1965 Winston Churchill dies. 750th anniversary of British Magna Carta. Edward Heath becomes the head of the British Conservative party.

1967 Jeremy Thorpe elected leader of British Labour party.

1972 Richard Nixon reelected U.S. president. A 47-day coal strike cripples Great Britain. Ireland, Britain, and Denmark agree to full participation in the European Economic Community (Common Market).

1974 British Prime Minister Heath resigns; Labour party leader Harold Wilson succeeds him. Terrorism continues in Northern Ireland. The Tower of London and the Houses of Parliament are bombed.

1975 Margaret Thatcher becomes leader of the British Conservative party, succeeding Edward Heath.

1977 Queen Elizabeth II celebrates her silver jubilee.

1979 Mrs. Thatcher becomes prime minister. Airey Neave is killed by a terrorist bomb.

1980 Unemployment high in Britain. Mrs. Thatcher maintains her support with the Conservative party. Ronald Reagan is elected president of the U.S.

1982 Argentina announces it has seized the Falkland Islands. Britain moves a flotilla of ships in immediately and beats the Argentines.

1983 Margaret Thatcher wins reelection.

1984 Irish Republican army makes unsuccessful attempt to kill Mrs. Thatcher and her cabinet at Brighton Conservative party conference. President Reagan is reelected in the U.S.

1985 Mikhail S. Gorbachev becomes the Soviet leader.

1987 Prime Minister Thatcher meets with Gorbachev. Thatcher is reelected, becoming the first British prime minister in the twentieth century to win three consecutive terms.

1988 George Bush is elected president of the U.S.

1989 For the first time in 70 years, the Soviet people are given a choice of competing candidates. The domino theory works in Eastern Europe as communism is rejected by country after country.

INDEX- *Page numbers in boldface type indicate illustrations.*

119

About the Author

Lelia Merrell Foster is a lawyer, United Methodist minister, and clinical psychologist with degrees from Northwestern University and Garrett Evangelical Theological Seminary. She is the author of books and articles on a variety of subjects.

Her interest in the ways that women function in different careers and her own heritage from a Methodist family in England made Margaret Thatcher an obvious choice for study. As a lawyer, Dr. Foster has served on a number of interprofessional bar association committees. As a psychologist, she has studied the role of women in public service.

Dr. Foster has made a number of trips to England and one coincided with one of Mrs. Thatcher's election campaigns. In this book, Dr. Foster has traced Mrs. Thatcher's career from chemist to tax lawyer to member of Parliament and ultimately the prime minister of Great Britain, with the longest term in office in the twentieth century.